APOPHTHEGMATA

St. Marcarius the Great,
Abbot of Scetis

Translated by: D.P. Curtin

Dalcassian
Publishing
Company

APOPHTHEGMATA

Copyright @ 2023 Dalcassian Publishing Company

All rights reserved. No part of this publication may be reproduced, distributed, or transmitted in any form or by any means, including photocopying, recording, or other electronic or mechanical methods, without the prior written permission of the publisher, except in the case of brief quotations embodied in critical reviews and certain other non-commercial uses permitted by copyright law. For permission request, write to Dalcassian Publishing Company at dalcassianpublishing at gmail.com

ISBN: 979-8-8691-2878-2 (Paperback)

Library of Congress Control Number:
Author: Curtin, D.P. (1985-)

Printed by Ingram Content Group, 1 Ingram Blvd, La Vergne, Tennessee

First printing edition 2023.

APOPHTHEGMATA

APOPHTHEGMATA

APOPHTHEGMATA

Some of the brothers asked Abbot Macarius the Great, inquiring what he was, and in what was 'perfection'? The old man answered and said: "A man must acquire great humility, which he not only holds in his heart, but also prefers in his body; esteeming himself in no way, but rather lowering every creature below him with a modest sense of self; by never judging anyone at all except himself; suffering insults, casting out of his heart all malice, making strength for himself to this end, that he may be long-suffering, kind, loving of his brethren, sober, chaste, self-controlled." For it is written: "The kingdom of heaven is of those who work for themselves."

"Rightly using the eyes, to see only those things that help the soul, watching over the guarding of the tongue, and turning away their ears from all vain and hurtful hearing, and holding hands so that they do nothing but just work. By keeping the heart pure before God, and the body undefiled, and having daily before his eyes the memory of death. He must deny inwardly anger and malice in the Spirit, but outwardly matter and sensible things, also related according to the flesh and at the same time pleasures; renouncing the devil and all his works; by praying to these things without ceasing, and in every time, place, business, and work, by attending to God, feeling that he is present, and venerating him. Unless one, I say, has done all these things, he cannot be perfect."

A certain brother, asking the old man, said: "Abba, what happens that, when I do all that is proper in my cell, I still do not find consolation from God?"

The old man said to him: "This happens to you because you indulge in vain and idle chatter; and because you want to be completely controlled by wishing your own will."

He answered the old man: "What then do you command me to do, father?"

The old man answered: "Go, enter into intimacy with a God-fearing man, and humble yourself before him; and surrender to your will; and then you will find comfort from God." Said the old man: "He that entereth into a sepulcher, and walketh in the market of perfumers, though he buys nothing, or come into contact with spices, nevertheless enjoys the fragrance altogether and in the meantime, and he himself smells well for a while: so, he that converses with the fathers, draws from them a salutary contagion which benefits him. If indeed he wishes to act rightly, he sees the way of humiliation pointed out to him by them; and the examples and words of these are like those walls to ward off the incursions of demons." The old man said: "If infirmity of body overtakes you, do not be troubled by giving yourself to inert sadness. For if your Lord wants you to be afflicted with a bodily disease, who are you to dare to be inflamed or to bear it painfully? Does he not take care of you in everything? Or can you live without him? therefore bear patiently: and pray to him that he may give you what he knows how to do. For this is his will. Sit with patience, eat charity." The old man said: "If a man had a keen nature to compete legitimately, God demands of him that he should not cling too much to anyone's bodily matter with affection, even to a minute needle; for if he loves anything like this more addicted, his mind will be hindered from the feelings and wishes worthy of God, through the intensity of the longing that is incubating the possessed; and the grief which he will experience from the loss of beloved things, by frequent and inevitable accidents." Said the old man: "Prayer, and a sober and attentive mind, and at the same time physical exertion, with abundant care persistently offered to God, equip a man with power for disturbances."

The old man was asked: "What does it mean for a man to live as a guest and a stranger?"

"Say", he said, to you; "Be silent, and I have no business here. Repeat and do this in every place and operation; then you will truly be in the state of a stranger and a stranger". The old man said: "A holy life without doctrine produces better than doctrine without a holy life. For a saint who is unlearned or silent is beneficial to those who see: a learned man without holiness, even if he only thinks, causes confusion. But if a sound doctrine and a holy life meet together, they complete the true and full appearance of the whole philosophy." Said the old man: "Do not aspire, or willingly accept to be the head of a congregation of brothers, lest you perhaps place on your neck the burdens of other people's sins". The same old man said: "To make one's strength in prayer, and to endure drought patiently for a long time, gives birth, to pray with joy and with rest. To make one's strength belongs to the strength of a good purpose: but to pray with quietness is a gift of grace."

APOPHTHEGMATA

ON THE ABBOT MACARIUS OF EGYPT.

[1] Abbot Macarius narrated about himself in this way: "When I was young and I was living in a cell in Egypt, they seized me and made me a cleric in the village; but unwilling to rest, I fled to another place. A pious man of all ages came to me, who accepted that I was working with my hands, and ministered to me. And it happened, through temptation, that a certain virgin fell by force into rape. When she was carrying the womb, it was asked, who was the author of the crime? So, he replied that he was from the port of Alexandria. Whence they came out, and seized me, and brought me to the village; and they hung pots infected with soot by the necks with the handles of the vessels, and thus they led me around the village through the streets, beating me and saying: This monk has corrupted our virgin; head him, head and they beat me almost to death. But an old man approaching, said: 'How long will you kill that foreign monk?' But he who ministered to me followed behind me, full of shame; for they had insulted him with many insults, saying: 'Behold, the anchorite, to whom you bore witness, what did he do?' To this the parents of the girl say: 'We will not let him go until he gives surety that he is going to feed her.' So, I signaled it to my servant, and he vouched for me. Afterwards he went to my cell, and I gave him the baskets that I had, saying: 'Sell and bring food to my wife.' Then with me: 'Macarius, behold, you have found a wife for yourself; you must work a little harder to nurture her'. And I worked night and day and sent it to him. Moreover, when the time came for the poor woman to give birth, she remained in torment for many days, and did not give birth. They asked, 'what was this?' She answered: 'I know that I have slandered the anchorite and accused him of lying; for he is not in fault, but he is a young man.' Then he who ministered to me, coming joyfully, announced: 'That virgin could not submit, until she thus confessed: The anchorite is beyond fault; but I have lied against him, and behold, the whole village wants to come here with honor, to demand forgiveness from you'. When I heard these things, lest the people should trouble me, I arose, and fled hither to Scetis. Hence my coming here has its beginning and cause.

APOPHTHEGMATA

[2] One day Macarius the Egyptian came from Scetis to the mountain of Nitra as an offering to Abbot Pambo, and the old men said to him: Deliver a sermon to the brethren, father. Then he said, I have not yet become a monk, but I have seen monks. For sometimes, sitting in the cell at Scetis, I was troubled by thoughts of going into the wilderness, and see what there meets your eyes. And I persevered for five years, fighting against the thought, lest perhaps I should be possessed by demons. And as the thought continued, I went into the desert. There I found a pool with an island in the middle of it, and the wild beasts were coming to it to drink. Between which I saw two naked men, and my body trembled: for I thought they were spirits. But when they saw me trembling, they said thus: Fear not, we are also men. I said to them: Where are you from, and how did you come into this wilderness? They answered: We are from the convent, and having come here by mutual consent, behold, forty years have passed since. One of us is Egyptian, the other Libyan. They also asked me in these words: How is the world? Did the water come in its season? Does the world get its usual abundance? I answered: Yes. In turn I inquired: By what means can I become a monk? They say to me: Unless one renounces all the things of the world, one cannot become a monk. I cried out: I am weak, and I cannot do as you do. They also answered: If you cannot, like us, sit in your cell and blow away your sins. I asked them, when is the winter, don't you have whales? When it is hot, does your body not burn? They answered, God has used this dispensation towards us, so that we shall not be cold in the winter, nor the heat hurt us in the summer. Therefore, I told you that I had not yet become a monk but had seen monks. Forgive me, brothers.

[3] When the abbot Macarius dwelt in Panerem, or all manner of solitude: but there alone he led the life of an anchorite, but below there was another desert, in which several brethren dwelt. At that time, I say, an old man of the place, looking round by the way, saw Satan coming in the shape of a man, to pass through the place where he was: but he appeared as if he were wearing a tunic with a perforated line, from the holes of which hung small boats. The great old man said to him: Where are you going? He answered: I am going to the brothers to suggest to them. Then the old man: And why do you have these bottles? He: I bring the broth to the brothers. Old man: And all this? He accepted, even if one thing did not please anyone, I would offer another; if not this, I will give him something else, but absolutely at least one of them will

please him. And with these words he went away. But the old man remained, observing the roads, until he returned. And as he looked at him, he said: Be safe. He answered: How can it happen to me that I may be saved? The old man? Why, he: Because they were all merciless to me, and not one supported me. To him the old man: Then you have no friend there? To the old man Satan: I have not one friend there, who even himself obeys me; as soon as he sees me, he turns like the wind. Then the old man: What is that brother called? Satan to this, Theopemtus. With this he departed. And so Abbot Macarius got up and went to the lower desert. And when the brothers learned of this fact, taking branches of palm trees, they came out to meet him. Moreover, every one of them prepared himself, thinking that the old man was going to make a difference with him. But he inquired who was on the mountain, who was called Theopemtus. When he found it, he went into his room. But Theopeptus received him with joy. And as he began to have alone with him, the old man: How, said he, are your affairs, brother? He says: Right, through your prayers. And the old man: Do your thoughts attack you? Him: In the meantime, I am fine. For he was ashamed to publish it. The old man said to him: Behold, for how many years I have led an ascetic life, and I am honored by all; but let the old spirit of fornication tear me away. Theopeptus accepted: Believe, Abba, me too. But the old man pretended to be assailed by other thoughts as well, until he brought him to confession. Afterwards he says to him: How do you fast? He answered: At nine o'clock. Then the old man: Fast until the evening, exercise yourself, meditate, and recite by heart from the Gospel and other Scriptures; whenever a thought overtakes you, you never look down, but always up; and the Lord will immediately provide you with help. And after the old man had informed his brother, he returned to his solitude. When he was watching, he saw that demon again, and said to him: Where are you going again? The brothers, he said, were instigated. And he is gone. As the old man passed by again, having torn him apart, how could the brothers have it? He answered: Badly. And the old man: Why? Demon: All are fierce; and what is worse, he, whom I had as a friend and obedient to me, he also, I do not know, has returned, and is no longer persuaded by me, but has become more ferocious than all: whence I swore that I would not tread those places again, except after a time. Having said this, he departed, leaving the old man. Then the saint entered his cell.

[4] Abbot Macarius the great came to Abbot Antonius on the mountain; and when he had knocked at the door, he came out and asked: Who are you? And he said: I am Macarius. And the door being shut, he went in, leaving him. But when he recognized his patience, he opened it. And dealing with him politely, he said: I have longed to see you for a long time, having heard your report. And being hospitably received, he refreshed himself, for he was weary from much labour. But when evening came, Abbot Antonius wetted branches of palm trees for himself. Abbot Macarius said to him: Order and I will dip myself. He said: Dip it. And having made a great bundle, he wove it. Therefore, sitting down in the evening, after talking about the salvation of souls, they plaited; and he went down through the window into the cave. And in the morning the blessed Anthony, coming in, saw the quantity of braids of the Abbot Macarius, and said: Much virtue proceeds from these hands.

[5] Abbot Macarius preached to the brethren about the devastation of the Sceteans: When you have looked at the cell built near the marsh, know that the desolation of the Sceteos is near: when you see the trees, it is at the doors; But when you have seen the children, take off your coats and depart.

[6] He said again, wanting to console the brothers: A child came hither with his mother, who was tormented by a demon, and said to his mother: Get up, old woman, let us go hence. But she said: I cannot walk on my feet. Then the boy said to her: I will carry you. And I marveled at the wickedness of the demon, how he wanted to drive them away from here.

[7] The Abbot Sisos reported: When I was in Scetis with Macarius, we went up seven names or men, that we might reap with him: and behold, a widow was gathering some ears of corn for us and did not cease to weep. Then the old man called the owner of the estate, and said to him: What does this old woman have that she is always crying? He answered: Because her husband, while he was keeping someone's deposit, died suddenly, and did not say where he had deposited it, and the owner of the deposit wants to claim her and her children as his slaves. The old man welcomed him. Tell him to come to us, where we rest because of the heat. And when the woman came, the old man said to her: Why are you crying so? She answered: My husband, having received the deposit,

departed from life, and dying did not indicate where he had laid. Then the old man said to her: Come, show me where you will bury him. So he took his brothers with him and went out with her. When they arrived at the place, the old man said to the woman: Go back to your house. And after they had prayed, the old man called the dead man with these words: He, where did you put the deposit of another? The man answered: It is hidden in my house, under the foot of the bed. The old man said to him: Sleep again until the day of resurrection. When the brothers saw this, they fell at his feet in fear. Then the old man said to them: This did not happen because of me, for I am nothing. But for the sake of the widow and orphans, God did the thing, and this is great, because God wants the soul to be without sin, and whatever it asks for it will receive. He therefore went forth and told the widow where the deposit lay. Taking it, he gave it to his master, and set the children at liberty, and all who heard the miracle gave glory to God.

[8] Abbot Peter told of the blessed Macarius, that when he once came to a certain anchorite and found him sick, he wondered what food he wanted to take: for there was nothing in his cell. After he had said, "a little cake," he did not hesitate to set out for Alexandria, a strong man, to give it to the patient.

[9] He mentioned again; Some have said to Abbot Macarius, who conversed with all his brethren in simplicity? Why do you show yourself like that? He answered: I have served my Lord for twelve years, that he might grant me this grace; and all have given me advice, should I put it down?

[10] They said of the Abbot Macarius, that if he spent his free time with his brethren, he would arrange it with him; if he brought wine for the sake of the brothers, drink it; and for one cup of wine, you shall not drink water for one day. Therefore, the brothers, desiring to restore it, gave it to him. But the old man admitted with joy that he might torture himself. But his disciple, to whom the matter was known, said to his brothers: By the Lord, do not give it to him; otherwise, he will finish himself in the cell. When the brothers discovered this, they no longer reached out to him.

[11] On one occasion Abbot Macarius, proceeding from the swamp to his cell, carried branches of palm trees; and behold, a devil carrying a scythe met him on the road. And as he wished to strike him, he could not. And so he said to him: You want a lot from you, Macarius, because I have no power against you. For whatever you do, I also do. You abstain from food, and I: you watch; I do not sleep at all. There is only one thing in which you beat me. Abbot Macarius asked: What is that? He answered: Your humility. And therefore, I can do nothing against you.

[12] Some of the fathers questioned the Abbot Macarius the Egyptian, saying: Who is it that, whether you eat or fast, your body is equally dry? And the old man answered them: The wood that covers the branches that are burned is completely consumed by the fire. In the same way, if a man has purified his mind in the fear of God, the very fear of God consumes his body.

[13] At one time Abbot Macarius went from Scetis to Terenuti; and he entered the barn to sleep. Now there were ancient corpses of ethnic groups; of which he placed one receipt under his head, like an embryo. The demons, therefore, seeing his audacity, were led to envy: and wishing to terrify him, they called him by name, as it were a woman, saying, "She, come with us to the bath." . But the old man was not afraid, but boldly beat his body: Arise, silent one, go into the darkness if you can. Hearing this, the demons cried out with a loud voice: You have defeated us. Then, filled with shame, they fled.

[14] They said of the Abbot Macarius the Egyptian, that, coming up from Scetis, and carrying his sackcloth, he sat down exhausted, and prayed to God in this manner: you know that I have no strength left. And immediately he was brought to the side of the river.

[15] A certain man in Egypt had a paralytic son, and he took him to the cell of Abbot Macarius; but leaving him weeping at the door, he went far away. So, the old man looked down and saw the boy, and asked him: Who brought you here? He answered: My father threw me here and went away. The old man says

to him: Get up and catch him. Immediately he recovered his health, he got up and followed his father: and so, they returned to their house.

[16] Abbot Macarius the great said to the brethren in Scetis, after he had dismissed the Church: Flee, brethren. Some of the elders said to him; How shall we escape beyond this wilderness? But he himself put his finger to his mouth, saying: Run away from this. Then he went into his room and sat with the door closed.

[17] Abbot Macarius said the same thing: If, by rebuking someone, you are moved to anger, you satisfy your affection. For you do not lose yourself in order to save others.

[18] The same Abbot Macarius, while he was in Egypt, found a man who had an animal, and was preying on what he possessed for his own use. "We brought nothing into the world: there is no doubt that we cannot take anything away. The Lord gave: as he willed, so it was done. Blessed be the Lord in all things."

[19] Some questioned Abbot Macarius, saying: How should we pray? The old man answered: There is no need to speak much, but they are to stretch out their hands and say: Lord, as you will and as you know, have mercy. But if the attack of temptation falls, it must be said: Lord, help. He knows what is expedient and has mercy on us.

[20] Abbot Macarius said, if contempt exists with you as praise, poverty as wealth, want as abundance, you will not die. For it cannot be that he who believes rightly and works in piety should fall into the filth of vices and the error of demons.

[21] They reported: Two brothers had sinned in Scetis, whom Abbot Macarius Urbicus had isolated or excommunicated, and some came and told Abbot Macarius the great Egyptian. He affirmed that the brothers were not separated, but Macarius; indeed, she loved him. When Abbot Macarius heard that he had

been excommunicated by the old man, he fled to the marsh. Abbot Macarius the great went out and found him pierced by gnats; and he says to him: You have separated the brothers, and they are going to retire to the village. But I set you apart; and you, like a beautiful virgin, fled into the inner chamber. But I, having called the brothers, learned from them that none of these things had happened. Take care, therefore, brother, that you are not deceived by demons. For you have seen nothing. But bow down and ask for forgiveness for your offense. And he said: If you will, give me penance. When the old man saw his humility, he said: Go, fast for three weeks, eating once every week. This, of course, was his continuous operation, fasting for weeks.

[22] Abbot Moyses said to Abbot Macarius in Scetis: I want to live in peace and silence, and my brothers do not allow me. Abbot Macarius said to him: I see that you are of a milder disposition and cannot turn your brother away from you: but if you long for a quiet life, go to the desert, enter into the rock, and dwell there quietly. And this he did and rested.

[23] The brother met Abbot Macarius the Egyptian and said to him: Abba, make me a word by what means I shall be saved. The old man said: Go to the tomb and attack the dead with curses. The brother, therefore, going away, desired abuses and stones: and he returned and announced to the old man. He asked him; Did they not answer you? Brother: Nothing. Then the old man said: To set out again to-morrow, bring them forth with praise. The brother therefore went on, and praised them, calling them: Apostles, holy, righteous. Then he went to the old man and said: I praised. He said to him: Did they answer you nothing? Brother: No way. Then the old man added: You know how many insults you have inflicted on them, and they have not spared you anything; and with how many praises you have adorned them, and they have spoken nothing to you; do not consider the insults of men, nor their praises, like the dead, so that you may be saved.

[24] On one occasion Abbot Macarius was passing through Egypt together with his brothers and heard a boy speaking thus to his mother: Mother, a certain rich man loves me, and I hate him; But the poor man hates me, and when I love him. Abbot Macarius was surprised when he heard this speech.

APOPHTHEGMATA

The brothers said to him: What is the meaning of this word, father, that you are moved with wonder? The old man answered them: Truly our Lord is rich and loves us, and we do not want to obey him; but our enemy the devil is poor, and pursues us with hatred, and we love his impurity.

[25] Abbot Poemen besought him with many tears, saying: Speak to me a word, how I shall attain salvation. But the old man answered him: What are you looking for? He has now withdrawn from the monks.

[26] On one occasion the Abbot Macarius met the Abbot Antonius, and having spoken to him, he returned to Scetis. The fathers went forward to meet him. And in the conversation the old man said to them: I told Abbot Anthony that in our place we lacked the offering. The fathers began to discuss other matters and did not seek to learn the answer from the old man, nor did the old man speak to them. Therefore some of the fathers pronounced this: When they see the fathers slip out of the memory of the brethren, that they may ask about matters useful to them, they impose upon themselves the necessity of bringing forth the principle of prayer: that if they are not addressed by the brethren, they do not pursue the conversation; so that they may not be caught speaking or questioned, and it may appear to be idle talk.

[27] Abbot Esa asked Abbot Macarius in this manner: Give me a sentence. And the old man said to him: People flee. Again, Abbas Esaa Aas: What is the point of fleeing people? But the old man: Sit in your cell and breathe out your sins.

[28] Abbot Paphnutius, a disciple of Abbot Macarius, reported this: I asked my father to tell me something. And his prayer was: You have injured no one, you have condemned no one. Observe these things and you will be saved.

[29] Abbot Macarius said: Do not sleep in the cell of a brother who has a bad reputation.

[30] One day the brothers came to Abbot Macarius Scetis, who was acting, and found nothing in his cell except rotten water. They say to him: Abba, go up into the village, we will restore you. The old man answered: Do you know, brothers, the bakery of such a man in the village? Answer: Yes. Then the old man: I also know. Do you also know his property, where the river jumps? They say, We know. I know it too, said the old man. When it pleases me, I do not have your work, but I bring it to myself.

[31] They said of Abbot Macarius, that if a brother approached him, with fear, as if to a holy and great old man, he said nothing to him. But if he should say to any of his brothers as if he were doing nothing; Abba, when you were a camel driver and you stole soda and sold it, didn't the guards beat you? If anyone had spoken to her, she would have given him an answer with joy, if he had asked anything.

[32] Of Abbot Macarius the Great they asserted that there existed, as it is written, an earthly God. Because as God covers the world; thus, Abbot Macarius covered up his offences; which he had won, as if he had not seen; what he had heard, as if he had not heard it.

[33] There is a story of the Abbot of Vitimius, which Abbot Macarius reported thus: While I was sitting one day in Scetis, two young pilgrims came down there; one of whom was wearing a beard, while the other was shedding the first down. They came to me asking, where was the cell of Abbot Macarius? Then I: What do you want him? They say: Having heard the report of him and the Sceteos, we came to see him. I say: I am. And having made an inclination of the body, they say: We wish to remain in this place. But I, seeing that they were nice and brought up as if in wealth, said to me: You cannot reside here. Then the elder said: If we cannot stay here, let us go to another place. I inside my mind; Why do I drive them away, and suffer them to be offended? The work will be done, so that they will flee of their own accord. And so I say to them: Come, build yourselves a cell, if you can. They: Show us a place and we will build. And the old man gave them an axe, and a bag full of bread and salt, and pointed out a hard rock, saying: Cut stones here, and bring wood from the swamp, and put a roof on it, and settle down. But I thought, says he, that they would retire

because of their labor. They further asked me what they were doing in that place. I answered, let them make a plait: and taking palm-leaves from the swamp, he showed them the beginning of the plait or rope, and that it was necessary to sew it; And I said: Make baskets, which you will hand over to the guards, but they will bring us bread. Then I went away. But they patiently carried out whatever I had ordered: they did not come to me for three years. But I constantly wrestled with my mind, considering; What is their activity, that they did not come to ask about the thought? Those who live at a distance come to me: and these, being near, did not approach, nor did they go to the others: they only went to the church, in silence, to receive the offering. Therefore, I prayed to the Lord, fasting for one week; to make it clear to me what they were working on. After a week, however, rising up, I went to them to observe how they were doing. And when I knocked, they opened, and greeted me with silence. I made a prayer and sat down. The elder beckoned to the younger to go out: he himself sat down, bent over to prepare, and said nothing. But at the ninth hour he made a noise. The younger came, made a little polenta, and, at the sign of the elder, set up the table, and having placed three paximates on it, stood silent. But I said: Get up, let us eat. Then we got up and took food. He brought a bowl, and we drank. But when the evening came, they asked me: Are you going back? I answered: No, but I sleep here. Wherefore they put a store for me on one side, and on the other side for themselves at another corner; they took their girdles and girdles and placed themselves together on the mat before me. Moreover, after they had composed themselves, I prayed to God to reveal to me their operation. Then the roof was opened, and light arose, as if by day; but they themselves did not see the light. But when they thought that I was asleep, the greater digs the side of the smaller, they rise, gird themselves, spread their hands to heaven. Furthermore, I saw them; they did not see me. At this I saw demons like flies coming upon the minor, some of whom approached to sit in his mouth, others in his eyes. At the same time, I saw the Angel of the Lord with a sword of fire in his hands, surrounding him, and driving the demons from him. But they could not approach the greater. About the time of the morning, however, they lay down; and they are likewise. And while this was spoken to me, a greater word was spoken: Do you want us to recite the twelve psalms? Accept: Yes. Then the minor sang five psalms, from six verses, and one alleluia, and at each verse, flames of fire issued from his mouth and ascended into heaven. In like manner also the greater one, when he opened his mouth in singing, came forth like a cord of fire, and reached up to heaven. I also recited from memory for a while. After that, going out, I said: Pray for me. But they bowed down in silence. I found, therefore, that although the elder was perfect, the enemy would still attack the younger. Moreover, after a few days, the elder brother fell asleep in the sleep of death, and on the third day afterwards the younger. And when some of the fathers went to Abbot Macarius, he led them into their cell, with these words: Come, see the martyrdom of the lesser pilgrims.

[34] Once upon a time the elders of the mountain sent to Abbot Macarius, who was standing in Scetis, beseeching him, and saying: Lest the whole multitude grow weary in coming to you, we pray you to come to us, where we may see, before you emigrate to the Lord. When he had come to the mountain, all the multitude gathered around him. But the elders asked him to speak to the brethren. When he heard the request, he said: Let us weep, and let our eyes fill with tears, before we go there, where our tears are to burn our bodies. And they all wept, and fell on their faces, and said: Father, pray for us.

[35] Another time the demon rose again against Abbot Macarius with a sword, wanting to cut off his foot: but when he could not because of his humility, he said to him: Whatever you have, we also have, only by humility are you put off from us and overcome.

[36] Abbot Macarius said: If we retain the memory of the evils that are inflicted upon us by men, we shall abolish the power of the remembrance of God: for if we were to remember the evils that befall us through demons, we shall be invulnerable.

[37] Abbot Paphnutius, a disciple of Abbot Macarius, reported the words of the old man: When I was a boy, I used to feed cattle with other boys; and they carried on the stolen figs. As they were running, one of them fell, which I picked up and ate. Every time, therefore, the memory of his incident returns, I sit weeping.

[38] The Abbot Macarius narrated: I was once traveling through the desert and found the skull of a dead man lying on the ground, which I had moved with the palm of my staff, the skull spoke to me. I say to him: Who are you? Caluaria answered me: I was the pontiff of the idols, and of their gentiles, who dwelt in this place: but you are Macarius, who bear the Spirit of God: at whatever hour you were moved by compassion for those who are engaged in torments, they feel little consolation. Said the old man: Which is consolation, and which is torture? As far as heaven is from the earth, says he, so much is the fire below us, standing from feet to head in the midst of the fire: and it is not permitted to see anyone face to face; but each one's face would cling to the other's back. So, when you pray for us, one looks at the face of the other from one side. This is comfort. And the old man, weeping, said: Woe to the day in which man was born! He added: Is there any other punishment more severe? The skull reported: A greater punishment is beneath us. Then the old man: And who lives there? He accepted: We, as those who did not know God, obtain mercy in a small way: but those who knew God and denied him are below us. Then the old man took the skull and ordered it on the ground.

[39] It is said of the Abbot Macarius the Egyptian that he once ascended the mountain of Nitra from Scetis, and as he stood near the place, he said to his disciple: Go ahead a little. And as he was going on, he met a certain priest of the Greeks or of the Gentiles. To whom the brother, crying, called; Alas, alas, inquisitive, where are you running, demon? But he turned, struck him with blows, and left him half dead. And taking up the stick which he was carrying, he ran. When he had advanced a little, he met Abbot Macarius in the middle of the course, who said to him: Be safe, be safe, after your labor is done. He came to him in surprise and said: What good did you see in me, that you greeted me? Then the old man: Because I saw you tired with work, and you do not know that you are tired in vain. The priest also said: I am sorry for your greeting, and I know that you are from the side of God. But another bad monk, being approached, insulted me: therefore, I gave him the blows to death. And the old man recognized that he was speaking of his disciple. Then, seizing him by the feet, the priest spoke thus: I will not let you go unless you make me a monk. And they came up, where the monk was, and carried him to the church on the mountain. And when they saw the priest with him, they were amazed; and they made him a monk. And many Gentiles became Christians because of him.

Abbot Macarius asserted, therefore, that bad speech also makes good people evil, and good speech also makes bad people good.

[40] Of Abbot Macarius they mentioned that a thief had entered his cell during his absence. And when he had returned, he found the robber, who was loading the camel with his goods. He, therefore, entered the cell, took from the vessels, and loaded the camel with him. As soon as they had put in the baggage, the thief began to beat the camel, so that it would get up; nor did he rise. Abbot Macarius, seeing further that he would not rise, entered the cell and found a small hoe, which he dropped and put on the camel, saying: Brother, this is what the camel was looking for. But the old man, knocking him with his foot, said: Get up. And he arose at once and completed his journey a short while because of his speech. But he sat down again and did not rise until they had put down all the furniture. Then he went away.

[41] Abbot Aio asked Abbot Macarius thus: Tell me something. Abbot Macarius said to him: Flee men; sit in your cell and blow away your sins; nor did you love the speech of men; and he will obtain salvation for you.

LATIN TEXT

APOPHTHEGMATA

APOPHTHEGMATA

Quidam e fratribus interrogavit Abbatem Macarium magnum, exquirens quænam esset, et in quo sita perfectio? Respondens senex dixit: Nisi acquisierit homo humilitatem magnam, quam non solum corde teneat, sed et corpore præferat; in nulla re se ipsum æstimans, sed potius modico sui sensu deprimens infra omnem creaturam; non judicando unquam omnino quemquam nisi se solum; sufferendo contumeliam, ejiciendo ex corde suo omnem malitiam: vim sibi faciendo ad hoc, ut sit longanimis, benignus, fratrum amator, sobrius, pudicus, continens. Scriptum est enim: "Vim sibi facientium est regnum coelorum." Recte utendo oculis, ad videndum ea tantum quæ juvant animan, invigilando custodiæ linguæ; avertendisque auribus ab omni auditione vana et noxia. Manus tenendo ne quidquam nisi justum operentur. Cor mundum coram Deo servando, corpusque impollutum. Habendo quotidie præ oculis mortis memoriam: abnegando intus in Spiritu iram et malitiam, exterius autem materiam et res sensibiles, cognatos quoque secundum carnem simulque voluptates; renuntiando item diabolo et cunctis operibus ejus; ad hæc indesinenter orando, et in omni tempore, loco, negotio, opere, astando Deo, præsentemquæ sentiendo ac venerando illum. Nisi quis, inquam, hæc omnia fecerit, perfectus esse non potest. Frater aliquis interrogans senem dixit: Abba, quæ fit, ut, cum ego in mea cellula faciam cuncta quæ decent, tamen non inveniam consolationem a Deo? Ait illi senex: Hoc tibi contingit eo, quod vanis cum otioso confabulationibus indulges; et quia omnino vis potiri optato voluntatem tuam propriam. Reposuit seni: Quid igitur facere me jubes, pater? Respondit senex: Vade, ini familiaritatem cum viro timente Deum, et humilia te ipsum coram eo; et renuntia voluntati tuæ; et tunc invenies consolationem a Deo. Dixit Senex: Qui ingreditur seplasiam, et in foro unguentario deambulat, etsi nihil emat aut contingat ex aromatibus, omnino tamen et interim fruitur odore, et ipse bene olet aliquandiu: sic qui conversatur cum patribus, trahit ex illis contagione salutari quod ipsum juvet: nam si quidem velit recte agere, monstratam ad hoc ab illis viam humiliationis videt; et horum exempla, verbaque instar illi muri sunt ad arcendas dæmonum incursiones. Dixit Senex: Si te infirmitas occupet corporis, ne turberis dans te tristitiæ inerti. Si enim velit te Dominus tuus morbo corporeo affligi, tu quis es, qui succensere aut ægre ferre audeas? Nonne ipse tui curam in omnibus gerit? an sine ipso vel potes vivere? patienter ergo tolera: et ora ipsum, ut tibi quæ novit expedire præbeat. Hæc enim est voluntas ejus. Sede cum longanimitate, comede charitatem. Dixit senex: Si acrem homo naturam ad legitime certandum exerat, exigit ab eo Deus, ne affectu nimio inhæreat materiæ corporeæ cuiquam, usque ad minutam acum; nam si quid tale addictius amaverit, impedietur mens ejus a sensibus et votis Deo dignis, per vehementiam desiderii possessis incubantis; et moerorem quem ex amatarum rerum jactura, crebro inevitabiliter accidente, concipiet. Dixit senex: Oratio, et sensus sobrii attentique, simulque vexatio corporis, cum abundantiori diligentia Deo perseveranter oblata, in perturbationes potestate hominem instruunt. Interrogatus est senex: Quid est, vivere hominem tanquam hospitem et peregrinum? Dic, inquit, tibi; Tace, et non habeo hic negotium. Hæc itera et fac in omni loco et operatione; tunc eris vere in statu advenæ et peregrini. Dixit senex: Vita sancta sine doctrina, plura bona efficit, quam doctrina sine vita sancta. Nam sanctus indoctus vel tacens videntibus prodest: doctus sine sanctitate, etiam solum cogitans, obturbat. Si autem doctrina sana et vita sancta in unum concurrant, philosophiæ totius veram et plenam speciem absolvunt. Dixit senex: Ne ambias, aut libenter admittas caput fieri congregationis fratrum, ne forte imponas collo tuo alienorum onera peccatorum. Dixit idem senex: Vim sibi facere in orando, et ariditatem diu ferre patienter, gignit, orare cum gaudio et cum quiete. Vim sibi facere ad robur boni propositi pertinet: orare autem cum quiete munus est gratiæ.

DE ABBATE MACARIO AEGYPTIO.

[I] NARRAVIT de se ipso Abbas Macarius ad hunc modum: Quando eram juvenis, et in cella residebam in Aegypto, apprehenderunt me ac fecerunt clericum in vico; sed nolens acquiescere, fugi ad alium locum. Venit ad me sæcularis vir pius, qui accipiebat quod manibus operabar, et ministrabat mihi. Contigit autem per tentationem, ut quædam virgo vi prolapsa sit in stuprum. Ea cum uterum gereret, interrogabatur, quis esset auctor criminis? Respondit itaque Anachoretam esse. Unde egressi comprehenderunt me adduxeruntque ad vicum; atque appenderunt collo fuligine infectas ollas cum ansis vasorum, sicque circumduxerunt me in vico per compita, verberantes ac dicentes: Iste monachus vitiavit nostram virginem; capite eum, capite. Et percusserunt me pene ad mortem. Accedens vero aliquis senum, dixit: Quousque cæditis monachum istum peregrinum? Qui autem mihi ministrabat, sequebatur post me, pudore suffusus; multis quippe contumeliis eum affecerant, inquientes: Ecce Anachoreta, cui tu testimonium perhibebas, quid fecit? Ad hæc aiunt parentes puellæ: Non dimittemus eum, donec fidejussorem dederit, quod aliturus sit eam. Itaque significabam ministro illi meo, et spopondit pro me. Postea profectus ad cellam meam, dedi ei, quas habui, sportulas, dicens: Vende et affer cibum uxori meæ. Tum apud me: Macari, ecce tibi invenisti uxorem;

oportet, ut paulo amplius labores, quo nutrias eam. Et operabar nocte dieque, mittebamque ei. Porro cum advenit tempus miseræ, ut pareret, ad multos dies in cruciatibus permansit, nec pariebat. Percontantur, quid hoc esset? Illa respondit: Ego scio, quoniam Anachoretam calumniata sum, prolatoque mendacio accusavi; neque enim in culpa est, sed ille juvenis. Tunc qui ministrabat mihi, lætus adveniens nuntiavit: Virgo illa non potuit parere, donec ita confiteretur: Extra culpam est Anachoreta; sed mentita sum adversus eum, et ecce totus vicus huc accedere vult cum honore, ut veniam a te supplex postulet. His ego auditis, ne mihi molestiam parerent homines, surrexi, atque huc in Scetim fugi. Inde principium causamque habet meus hic adventus.

[II] Venit aliquando Macarius Aegyptius a Sceti ad montem Nitriæ in oblatione Abbatis Pambo, et dicunt ei senes: Sermonem profer fratribus, pater. Tum ille infit, ego nondum evasi in monachum, sed monachos vidi. Mihi namque aliquando sedenti in cella apud Scetim molestæ erant cogitationes proficiscere in solitudinem, et vide quid illic oculis tuis occurret. Perstiti autem quinque annis, pugnans adversus cogitationem, ne forte inquiens a dæmonibus sit. Utque perseveravit cogitatio, abii in eremum. Illic inveni stagnum cum insula in medio ejus, et ad illud veniebant bestiæ eremi, ut biberent. Quas inter conspexi duos homines nudos, et contremuit corpus meum: existimavi enim esse spiritus. Ipsi vero postquam me viderunt trementem, ita locuti sunt: Noli timere, etiam nos homines sumus. Dixi illis: Unde estis, et quomodo venistis in solitudinem hanc? Responderunt: E coenobio sumus atque ex mutuo consensu egressi venimus huc, ecce quadraginta abhinc anni præterierunt. Unus e nobis Aegyptius est, alter Libycus. Ipsi quoque interrogaverunt me, his verbis: Quomodo se habet mundus? Venit-ne aqua in tempore suo? Mundus obtinet-ne abundantiam solitam? Respondi: Etiam. Vicissim ego percontatus sum: Quanam ratione fieri potero monachus? Aiunt mihi : Nisi quis renuntiaverit omnibus mundi rebus, non potest fieri monachus. Excepi: Ego infirmus sum, nec possum sicuti vos. Exceperunt etiam illi: Si non potes, quemadmodum nos, sede in cella tua, et peccata tua defle. Quæsivi ab eis, quando hyems est, non algetis? Quando æstus est, non uritur corpus vestrum? Responsum dederunt, Deus erga nos hac usus est dispensatione, nec hyeme rigemus, nec æstate nos æstus lædit. Propterea dixi vobis me nondum in monachum evasisse, sed vidisse monachos. Ignoscite mihi, fratres.

[III] Abbas Macarius cum in paneremo, seu omnimoda solitudine habitaret: solus autem illic anachoreticam vitam ducebat, infra vero alia erat eremus, in qua plures fratres degebant. Eo, inquam, loci aliquando per viam circumspiciens senex, vidit Satanam venientem in figura hominis, ut per locum, in quo erat, transiret: apparebat autem quasi tunicam gestans lineam perforatam, a cujus foraminibus pendebant parvi lecythi. Dicit ei magnus senex: Quo vadis? Respondit: Proficiscor ad fratres, ut eis suggeram. Tum senex: Et quare tibi ampullæ hæ? Ille: Affero fratribus condimenta. Senex: Et hæc omnia? Excepit, etiam, si unum alicui non placuerit, aliud porrigo; si neque hoc, do aliud, omnino autem ex illis saltem unum placiturum est ei. Atque his dictis abiit. At senex remansit, observans vias, donec reverteretur. Utque conspexit illum, ait: Salvus sis. Ille respondit: Quomodo contingere mihi poterit, ut salvus sim? Senex? Quare, Ille: Quia cuncti mihi fuerunt immites, nec ullus sustinuit me. Ad eum senex: Nullus ergo illic tibi amicus? Ad senem Satanas: Ne unum ibi amicum habeo, qui vel ipse mihi obtemperat; cumque me conspicit, instar auræ vertitur. Tum senex: Quomodo vocatur frater ille? Satanas ad hoc, Theopemptus. Quo dicto discessit. Itaque surgens abbas Macarius perrexit ad inferiorem eremum. Eaque re comperta fratres, sumentes ramos palmarum, ei obviam prodierunt. Cæterum unusquisque eorum præparabat se, putans, quod apud ipsum diversaturus esset senex. At ille requisivit, quisnam esset in monte, qui Theopemptus appellaretur. Quo invento, intravit in cellam ejus. Theopemptus autem suscepit eum lætus. Utque coepit solum secum habere, senex: Quomodo, inquit, se res tuæ habent, frater? Is dicit: Recte, per preces tuas. Et senex: Num impugnant te cogitationes? Ille: Interim mihi bene est. Pudebat enim eum edicere. Ait illi senex: Ecce a quot annis vitam asceticam duco, et honore afficior ab omnibus; attamen me senem Spiritus fornicationis divexat. Theopemptus excepit: Crede, Abba, me etiam. Senex vero simulabat ab aliis etiam cogitationibus impugnari se, donec eum ad confessionem adduceret. Postea dicit ei: Quomodo jejunas? Respondit: Ad horam nonam. Tum senex: Jejuna usque ad vesperam, exerce te, meditarc, ac recita memoriter ex Evangelio aliisque Scripturis; cumque te subierit cogitatio, nunquam deorsum spectes, sed sursum semper; statimque tibi Dominus præbebit auxilium. Et postquam fratrem informasset senex, reversus est ad solitudinem suam. Ubi observans iterum videt dæmonem illum, atque ei: Quo iterum pergis? Fratres, inquit, instigatum. Atque abiit. Ut vero rursus transiit, sciscitatus illum senex, quomodo haberent fratres? Respondit: Male. Et senex: Cur? Dæmon: Cuncti feroces sunt; quodque pejus est, ille, quem habebam amicum, et obsequentem mihi, ipse etiam, unde nescio, reversus est, nec amplius a me persuadetur, sed cunctis ferocior evasit: unde juravi me amplius ea loca non calcaturum, nisi post tempus. Quo pronuntiato, discessit, senem relinquens. Tunc sanctus intravit in cellam suam.

[IV] Venit Abbas Macarius magnus ad Abbatem Antonium in montem; cumque pulsasset ostium, egressus est, petiitque: Tu quis es? Ille autem: Ego, inquit, sum Macarius. Et ostio clauso, intravit, relinquens eum. Sed postquam agnovit patientiam ejus, aperuit. Atque cum eo urbane agens, dixit: A multo tempore videre te desiderabam, audita tui fama. Et hospitaliter susceptum refecit, erat enim e multo labore fessus. Vespere autem facto, Abbas Antonius sibi madefecit ramos palmarum. Ait ei Abbas Macarius: Jube et ego mihi intinguam. Ille: Intingue, inquit. Confectoque magno fasciculo, intexit. Igitur sedentes a vespera, collocuti de animarum salute, plectebant; plecta autem per fenestram descendebat in speluncam. Et mane ingrediens beatus Antonius, vidit plectæ Abbatis Macarii copiam, et infit: Multa virtus e manibus istis egreditur.

[V] Abbas Macarius prædixit fratribus de vastatione Sceteos: Quando spectaveritis cellam ædificatam juxta paludem, scitote, quod prope sit Sceteos desolatio: quando videritis arbores, ad fores est; cum autem pueros conspexeritis, tollite melotes vestras, atque discedite.

[VI] Dixit iterum, volens fratres consolari: Venit huc cum matre sua puer, qui a dæmonio vexabatur, et dicebat matri: Surge anus, abeamus hinc. Illa vero: Non possum, inquit, pedibus incedere. Tum puer ad eam: Ego te portabo. Et admiratus sum dæmonis nequitiam, quomodo eos hinc voluisset fugare.

[VII] Referebat Abbas SisoÂˆÂ's: Quaudo eram in Sceti cum Macario, ascendimus septem nomina seu homines, ut cum eo meteremus: et ecce vidua quædam pone nos spicas colligebat, nec cessabat plorare. Vocavit ergo senex dominum prædii, dixitque ei: Quid habet anus hæc, quod semper plorat? Respondit: Quia vir ejus alicujus depositum dum servat, mortuus est subito, nec enuntiavit, ubi posuerit illud, vultque depositi dominus eam et liberos ejus sibi in servos vindicare. Excepit senex Dic ei ut veniat ad nos, ubi ob æstum conquiescimus. Cumque venisset mulier, ait illi senex: Quare omnino ita fles? Respondit illa: Maritus meus accepto deposito emigravit e vita, nec significavit moriens, ubi posuerit. Tunc senex ad eam: Veni, ostende mihi ubi sepelieris eum. Itaque ductis secum fratribus cum ea egressus est. Ut pervenerunt ad locum, dixit senex mulieri: Recede in domum tuam. Et postquam precati fuissent, vocavit senex mortuum his verbis: Ille, ubi posuisti alienum depositum? Responsionem dedit homo: Absconditum est in domo mea, sub pede lecti. Senex ad ipsum: Iterum dormi usque ad resurrectionis diem. Hoc videntes fratres, præ timore ceciderunt ad pedes ejus. Tum illis senex: Non propter me id evenit, nihil quippe sum: sed propter viduam et pupillos Deus rem fecit, hoc vero magnum est, quod Deus vult animam esse sine peccato, et quidquid petierit accipiet. Profectus ergo nuntiavit viduæ, ubi jaceret depositum. Quæ accipiens dedit domino, ac in libertatem asseruit liberos, omnesque qui miraculum audiverunt, gloriam dederunt Deo.

[VIII] Narravit Abbas Petrus de beato Macario, quod cum advenisset aliquando ad quemdam anachoretam, et invenisset eum ægrotantem, sciscitatus sit, quidnam cibi vellet sumere: nihil quippe erat in cella ejus. Qui postquam dixisset, pastillum, non piguit virum fortem Alexandriam proficisci, ut ægro daret: miraque res nemini manifesta facta est.

[IX] Iterum memoravit; Ad Abbatem Macarium cum fratribus cunctis in simplicitate conversantem dixerunt nonnulli? Quare te talem præbes? Ille respondit: Duodecim annos servivi Domino meo, ut mihi hanc gratiam largiretur; et omnes mihi consilium datis, uti eam deponam?

[X] Dicebant de Abbate Macario, quod si cum fratribus vacans versaretur, ita secum constituebat; si vinum affuerit propter fratres bibe; et pro uno vini poculo, per unum diem aquam non bibas. Igitur fratres, reficere cupientes, dabant ei. Senex autem cum gaudio admittebat, ut se ipsum torqueret. At discipulus ejus, cui res nota erat, dicebat fratribus: Per Dominum, ne præbeatis illi; alioqui in cella confecturus est se. Quo comperto fratres, non amplius ei porrigebant.

[XI] Proficiscens aliquando Abbas Macarius a palude in cellam suam, portabat palmarum ramos; et ecce occurrit ei in via diabolus falcem gerens. Utque voluit eum ferire, non valuit. Itaque ait ei: Multa a te vis, Macari, quod adversus te nihil valeo. En enim, quidquid agis, ego quoque facio. Tu cibo abstines, et ego: vigilas; ego penitus non dormio. Unum solum est in quo vincis me. Interrogavit

Abbas Macarius: Quodnam est illud? Respondit: Humilitas tua. Ac propterea adversus te nihil possum.

[XII] Interrogaverunt quidam e patribus Abbatem Macarium Aegyptium, dicentes: Qui fit, ut sive comedas, sive jejunes, corpus tuum pariter siccum sit? Responditque illis senex: Lignum quod versat sarmenta quæ comburuntur, omnino ab igne consumitur. Simili modo si mentem suam homo in timore Dei mundaverit, ipse Dei timor corpus ejus consumit.

[XIII] Profectus est aliquando Abbas Macarius a Sceti in Terenuthim; et ingressus est fanum, ut dormiret. Erant autem ibi vetera ethnicorum cadavera; e quibus unum acceptum posuit sub capite suo, velut embrimium. Dæmones ergo intuiti audaciam ejus, invidia ducti sunt: ac volentes eum terrere, velut foeminam de nomine vocabant, dicentes: Illa, veni nobiscum ad balneum: respondit autem alius dæmon sub ipso tanquam e mortuis, sic: Peregrinum habeo super me, nec possum venire. At senex territus non est, sed audacter verberabat corpus: Surge, inquiens, vade in tenebras si potes. Quo audito dæmones clamaverunt voce magna: Vicisti nos. Tum pudore suffusi aufugerunt.

[XIV] Dicebant de Abbate Macario Aegyptio, quod ascendens e Sceti, ac sportulas portans, defatigatus sedit, oravitque ad hunc modum Deus: tu scis, nihil mihi virium superesse. Et illico juxta fluvium est delatus.

[XV] Quidam in Aegypto filium habebat paralyticum, et tulit eum ad cellam Abbatis Macarii; relinquens autem ad ostium plorantem, longe abscessit. Igitur senex deorsum aspiciens vidit puerum, et interrogavit eum: Quis te huc attulit? Respondit: Pater meus hic me projecit, et abiit. Dicit ei senex: Surgens assequere eum. Statimque sanitate recuperata surrexit et patrem consecutus est: atqu ita reversi sunt in domum suam.

[XVI] Abbas Macarius magnus dicebat fratribus in Sceti, postquam Ecclesiam dimisisset: Fugite, fratres. Ait illi seniorum quidam; Quonam fugere poterimus ultra solitudinem hanc? Ipse vero digitum suum ad os ponebat, dicens: Fugite hoc. Tum ingrediebatur in cellam suam, et clauso ostio sedebat.

[XVII] Dixit idem Abbas Macarius: Si quempiam increpando, ad iram commoveris, affectui tuo satisfacis. Non enim, ut alios salves, perdes te ipsum.

[XVIII] Idem Abbas Macarius, dum esset in Aegypto, invenit hominem habentem jumentum, et prædantem quæ ad usum suum possidebat: ipse vero tanquam peregrinus astans furi, una onerabat jumentum, magnaque cum quiete deduxit eum, dicens; "Nihil intulimus in mundum: haud dubium quod nec auferre quid possumus. Dominus dedit: sicut ipse voluit, ita et factum est. Benedictus Dominus in omnibus."

[XIX] Interrogaverunt quidam Abbatem Macarium dicentes: Quomodo debemus orare? Respondit ille senex: Non opus est loqui multum, sed extendendæ sunt manus, proferendumque: Domine, sicut vis et sicut nosti, miserere. Si autem ingruerit tentationis impugnatio, dici debet: Domine, adjuva. Ipse scit, quæ expediant, et facit nobiscum misericordiam.

[XX] Dixit Abbas Macarius; Si apud te extiterit contemptus velut laus, paupertas tanquam divitiæ, indigentia sicut abundantia, non moreris. Fieri enim non potest, ut qui recte credit, et in pietate operatur, incidat in vitiorum sordes ac dæmonum errorem.

[XXI] Referebant: Duo fratres in Sceti deliquerunt, quos segregavit seu excommunicavit Abbas Macarius Urbicus, et venerunt nonnulli, nuntiaruntque Abbati Macario magno Aegyptio. Qui affirmavit fratres non esse segregatos, sed Macarium; etenim diligebat eum. Auditu accepit Abbas Macarius, quod a sene excommunicatus fuisset, fugitque ad paludem. Egressus itaque est Abbas Macarius magnus, ac reperit eum a culicibus perforatum; dicitque ei: Tu segregasti fratres, et secessuri sunt in vicum. Ego vero segregavi te; tuque, veluti pulchra virgo in interius cubiculum fugisti huc. At ego, vocatis fratribus, ab ipsis didici nihil horum factum esse. Vide igitur tu, frater, ne a dæmonibus illusus fueris. Nam nihil vidisti. Sed veniam incurvatus pete pro delicto tuo. Ille autem dixit: Si vis, da mihi poenitentiam. Videns ergo senex humilitatem illius, ait: Vade, jejuna tres hebdomadas, semel singulis hebdomadis comedens. Hæc scilicet erat illius perpetua operatio, hebdomadas jejunare.

[XXII] Dixit Abbas Moyses Abbati Macario in Sceti: Volo cum quiete ac silentio vivere, nec sinunt me fratres. Ait illi Abbas Macarius: Video te indolis mollioris esse, nec posse fratrem a te avertere: sed si desideras quietam vitam, proficiscere ad eremum, intro in petra, et illic quiete deges. Atque hoc fecit, et conquievit.

[XXIII] Frater convenit Abbatem Macarium Aegyptium, et dixit ei: Abba, effare mihi verbum, quonam modo salvus ero. Ait senex: Vade ad sepulcrum, et maledictis mortuos impete. Abiens igitur frater, conviciis et lapidibus appetiit: reversusque annuntiavit seni. Quærit ab eo; Nihil tibi responderunt? frater: Nihil. Tum senex inquit: Iterum proficiscere cras, laudibus eos effer. Pergens itaque frater, collaudavit eos, vocans: Apostoli, sancti, justi. Tum adiit senem dixitque: Laudavi. Ille ei: Nihil tibi responderunt? Frater: Nullo modo. Tunc senex infit: Nosti quantis eos contumeliis affeceris, nec quidquam reposuerunt tibi; et quantis eosdem laudibus ornaveris, nihilque ad te prolocuti sunt: ita etiam tu, si salutem consequi desideras, mortuus fias; nec injurias hominum, nec laudes eorum cogites, instar mortuorum, sic poteris salvus fieri.

[XXIV] Præteriens aliquando Abbas Macarius per Aegyptum una cum fratribus, audivit puerum ita matri suæ loquentem: Mater, quidam dives diligit me, et odi eum; pauper vero odit me, ac cum diligo. Quo audito sermone admiratus est Abbas Macarius. Dicunt ei fratres: Quid hoc verbi est, pater, quod affectus sis admiratione? Respondit illis senex: Revera Dominus noster dives est diligitque nos, nec volumus illi obtemperare; inimicus autem noster diabolus pauper est, odioque nos prosequitur, et diligimus ejus impuritatem.

[XXV] Rogavit eumdem multis cum lacrymis Abbas Poemen, dicens: Eloquere mihi verbum, quomodo assecuturus sim salutem. Senex vero ei respondit: Quam quæris rem, nunc recessit a monachis.

[XXVI] Aliquando Abbatem Antonium convenit Abbas Macarius, habitoque ad eum sermone, Scetin reversus est. Obviam ei processerunt patres. Et in colloquio ait illis senex: Abbati Antonio dixi, quod in loco nostro careamus oblatione. Coeperunt patres disserere aliis de rebus, nec requisierunt responsum discere a sene, nec senex eis prolocutus est. Hoc ergo pronuntiabat patrum quidam: Cum viderint patres, e fratrum memoria excidere, ut interrogent de re eis utili, necessitatem sibi imponunt principium orationis proferendi: quod si a fratribus non adigantur, non persequuntur sermonem; ut ne deprehendantur locuti neque interrogati, videaturque esse otiosa loquela.

[XXVII] Hunc in modum percontatus est Abbas Esaâ^Ã~s Abbatem Macarium: Profer mihi sententiam. Et dixit ei senex: Homines fuge. Rursus Abbas Esaâ^Ã~as: Quid est fugere homines. Senex vero: Sedere in cella tua, et deflere tua peccata.

[XXVIII] Hoc referebat Abbas Paphnutius discipulus Abbas Macarii: Rogavi patrem meum, ut aliquid mihi diceret. Illius autem oratio fuit: Neminem læseris, neminem condemnaveris. Hæc observa et salvus fies.

[XXIX] Dixit Abbas Macarius: Noli dormire in cella fratris, qui malam famam habet.

[XXX] Accesserunt aliquando fratres ad Abbatem Macarium Sceti agentem, nec quidquam invenerunt in cella ejus, nisi aquam putridam. Dicunt ei: Abba, ascende in pagum, reficiemus te. Excepit senex: Nostis, fratres, illius talis hominis pistrinum in pago? Respondent: Etiam. Tum senex: Ego quoque novi. Scitis et prædium illius, ubi fluvius salit? Aiunt; Scimus. Ego quoque scio, inquit senex. Quando igitur placet, vestri opus non habeo, sed mihi apporto.

[XXXI] Aiebant de Abbate Macario, quod si ad eum accederet frater, cum timore, tanquam ad sanctum et magnum senem, nihil ei loquebatur. Si vero fratrum quispiam tanquam nihili faciens ei diceret; Abba, quando eras camelarius, et nitrum furabaris, ac vendebas, nonne verberabant te custodes? Si ista quis esset prolocutus, huic cum gaudio, si quid interrogasset, responsum dabat.

[XXXII] De Abbato Macario Magno asserebant, quod extiterit, sicut scriptum est, Deus terrestris. Quia quemadmodum Deus mundum tegit; ita Abbas Macarius delicta obtegebat; quæ vicerat, quasi non vidisset; quæ audierat, quasi non audivisset.

[XXXIII] Narratio Abbatis Vitimii extitit, quod ita retulerit Abbas Macarius: Sedente me aliquando in Sceti, descenderunt illuc duo juvenes peregrini; quorum unus barbam gerebat, alter vero primam emittebat lanuginem. Hi venerunt ad me rogantes, ubi esset cella Abbatis Macarii? Tum Ego: Quid eum vultis? Aiunt: Audita ejus ac Sceteos fama, venimus, ut videamus eum. Dico: Ego sum. Factaque corporis inclinatione, inquiunt: Hoc in loco cupimus manere. Ego vero videns eos delicatos et velut in divitiis educatos, aio: Non potestis residere hic. Tum major infit: Si non possimus remanere hic, ad alium pergemus locum. Ego intra mentem meam; Cur pello eos, et scandalum patientur? Efficiet labor, ut ipsi sponte fugiant. Itaque dico eis: Venite, construite vobis cellam, si potestis. Illi: Ostende nobis locum, construemus. Dedit autem eis senex securim, peramque plenam panibus, et sal: ostenditque petram duram, monens: Lapides hic incidite, atque ex palude portate vobis ligna, tectoque imposito, residete. Putabam autem, inquit, illos propter laborem recessuros. Porro petierunt a me, quid eo loci operaturi essent. Respondi, plectam facerent: sumptisque e palude foliis palmarum, ostendi ipsis plectæ seu funis principium, utque consuere oporteret; dixique: Facite sportas, quas tradetis custodibus, ipsi vero afferent nobis panes. Deinde abscessi. At illi patienter quæcumque mandaveram executi sunt: nec venerunt ad me tribus annis. Ego vero assidue cum animo meo colluctabar, reputans; Ecquæ est eorum operatio, quod non accesserint interrogaturi de cogitatione? Qui procul habitant, veniunt ad me: et isti cum propinqui sint, non accesserunt, nec ad alios profecti sunt: duntaxat pergunt ad Ecclesiam, taciti, ut accipiant oblationem. Igitur oravi Dominum, jejunans una hebdomade; ut manifestum mihi faceret, quidnam operarentur. Post hebdomadam vero surgens, ad eos abii, ut intuerer, quomodo agerent. Et cum pulsassem aperuerunt, meque salutarunt cum silentio. Feci orationem, et sedi. Major innuit minori, ut egrederetur: ipseque sedit, ad conficiendam plectam, nec quidquam loquebatur. Ad horam vero nonam strepitum edidit. Venit junior, fecit parum polentæ, ac majore innuente apposuit mensam, cumque super eam tres paximates posuisset, stetit tacens. Ego vero dixi: Surgite, comedamus. Inde consurgentes cibum sumpsimus. Attulit baucale, ac bibimus. Ut autem advenit vespera, petunt a me: Recedis-ne? Respondi: Non, sed hic dormio. Unde posuerunt mihi stoream et parte, et sibi ad alium angulum ex parte; tuleruntque zonas suas et succinctoria, simulque collocaverunt se in matta ante me. Cæterum postquam composuerunt se, oravi Deum, ut mihi operationem eorum revelaret. Tunc apertum est tectum, ortaque est lux, velut per diem; ipsi autem non cernebant lucem. Cum vero existimarent dormire me, major fodicat minoris latus, Consurgunt, cingunt se, expandunt manus ad coelum. Porro ego cernebam eos; ipsi non videbant me. Ad hæc vidi dæmones instar muscarum venientes super minorem, quorum alii accedebant, ut sederent in ore ejus, alii in oculis. Simul conspexi Angelum Domini cum gladio ignis præ manibus, circumvallantem eum, dæmonesque ab eo propellentem. At majori non poterant appropinquare. Circa matutinum vero tempus, recubuerunt: ego assimilavi, me mox expergefactum; ipsique similiter. Hoc autem dumtaxat mihi elocutus est verbum major: Vis recitemus duodecim Psalmos? Excipio: Etiam. Tum psallit minor quinque Psalmos, a sex versibus, et unum alleluia, atque ad unumquemque versum, exibat ignis lampas ex ore ejus, ascendebatque in coelum. Pari modo etiam major, quando aperiebat os in psallendo, tanquam funiculus ignis egrediebatur, et pertingebat usque in coelum. Etiam ego parumper ex pectore ac memoria recitavi. Post quod exiens, dixi: Orate pro me. Ipsi autem inclinaverunt se, tacentes. Comperi ergo, quod major perfectus esset, minorem adhuc impugnaret inimicus. Cæterum post paucos dies, mortis somnum obdormivit major frater, ac tertia dein die minor. Cumque e patribus nonnulli adirent Abbatem Macarium, ducebat eos in istorum cellam, cum his verbis: Venite, videte martyrium minorum peregrinorum.

[XXXIV] Miserunt aliquando ad Abbatem Macarium in Sceti consistentem senes montis, orantes eum, et aiunt: Ne universa multitudo ad te veniendo fatigetur, precamur, ut accedas ad nos, quo videamus, antequam emigres ad Dominum. Qui ad montem cum affuisset, congregata est omnis multitudo circa eum. Senes vero rogaverunt, ut ad fratres haberet sermonem. Ille audita rogatione: Ploremus, inquit, et oculi nostri profundant lacrymas, antequam eo abeamus, ubi lacrymæ nostræ combusturæ sunt corpora nostra. Et ploraverunt cuncti, cecideruntque super faciem suam, necnon dixerunt: Pater, ora pro nobis.

[XXXV] Alia iterum vice dæmon insurrexit adversus Abbatem Macarium cum gladio, volens pedem ejus amputare: sed cum propter humilitatem ipsius non posset, dixit ei: Quæcumque habetis, habemus etiam nos: sola humilitate a nobis differtis et prævaletis.

[XXXVI] Dixit Abbas Macarius: Si retinuerimus memoriam malorum, quæ nobis inferuntur ab hominibus, abolemus vim recordationis Dei: quod si recordati fuerimus malorum quæ per dæmones contingunt, erimus invulnerati.

[XXXVII] Retulit Abbas Paphnutius, discipulus Abbatis Macarii, verba senis: Quando eram puer, cum aliis pueris pascebam buculas; et perrexerunt furatum ficus. Dumque currunt, una ex iis cecidit, quam tollens comedi. Quoties ergo ejus rei redit memoria, plorans sedeo.

[XXXVIII] Narravit Abbas Macarius: Iter agens aliquando per eremum, inveni calvariam mortui ad solum jacentem; quam cum palmeo baculo movissem, locuta mihi est calvaria. Dico ei: Tu quis es. Respondit mihi caluaria: Ego eram pontifex idolorum, eorumque gentilium, qui hoc loco morabantur: tu vero es Macarius, qui Spiritum Dei fers: quacumque hora commotus fueris misericordia erga eos, qui in tormentis versantur, exiguum sentiunt solatium. Ait senex: Quodnam est solatium, et quodnam tormentum? Quantum, inquit, a terra distat coelum, tantum est ignis infra nos, a pedibus ad caput stantibus nobis in medio ignis: nec licet facie ad faciem videre quemquam; sed cujusque facies dorso alterius adhæret. Quando igitur oras pro nobis, unus ex parte spectat faciem alterius. Hoc est solatium. Et flens senex, dixit: Væ diei in qua natus est homo! Addidit: Est-ne aliud gravius supplicium? Retulit cranium: Major poena est subter nos. Tum senex: Et quinam illic degunt? Excepit: Nos, utpote qui ignoravimus Deum, modice misericordiam consequimur: qui vero cognoverunt Deum, et negaverunt eum, subtus nos sunt. Tunc senex calvariam sumens, humo mandavit.

[XXXIX] Dictum est de Abbate Macario Aegyptio, quod aliquando e Sceti ascendebat in montem Nitriæ: et ut prope locum extitit, dixit discipulo suo: Præcede paululum. Cumque ille præiret, obvium habuit quemdam Græcorum seu gentilium sacerdotem. Ad quem clamans frater, vocabat; Heu, heu, inquiens, quo curris, dæmon? Ille vero conversus, plagas ei inflixit, reliquitque semimortuum. Ac tollens, quod portabat lignum, cucurrit. Paululum progresso occurrit inter cursum Abbas Macarius, qui dixit ei: Salvus sis, salvus sis labore confecte. Ille admiratus venit ad eum, et ait: Quid boni vidisti in me, quod me salutaveris? Tum senex: Quoniam conspexi te labore fessum, ac nescis te in vanum defatigari. Sacerdos quoque: Ego salutatione tua compunctus sum, et cognovi ex parte Dei te esse. Alius vero malus monachus, obvius factus, contumelia me affecit: quare ego dedi ei plagas ad mortem. Agnovit autem senex, quod de discipulo suo loqueretur. Tunc, apprehensis ejus pedibus, sacerdos ita locutus est: Non dimittam te, nisi me feceris monachum. Et venerunt sursum, ubi erat monachus, portaveruntque illum ad Ecclesiam montis. Porro cernentes sacerdotem cum eo, stupefacti sunt; et fecerunt illum monachum. Multique gentilium propter eum facti sunt Christiani. Asserebat ergo Abbas Macarius, quod sermo malus etiam bonos malos faciat, et sermo bonus etiam malos bonos.

[XL] De Abbate Macario memorabant, quod absente illo ingressus sit latro in cellam ejus. Cum autem rediisset, invenit latronem, qui camelum suppellectile sua onerabat. Ipse igitur intrans in cellam, de vasis accipiebat, et una cum eo onerabat camelum. Ut ergo sarcinam immiserunt, coepit fur verberare camelum, ut surgeret; neque surgebat. Videns porro Abbas Macarius, quod non exurgeret, cellam ingressus invenit parvum sarculum, emissumque imposuit camelo, dicens: Frater, hoc quærebat camelus. Pede vero pulsans eum senex, ait: Surge. Confestimque surrexit, et parumper itineris confecit propter ejus sermonem. Sed iterum resedit, nec exurrexit, donec deposuissent cunctam suppellectilem. Tunc enim abiit.

[XLI] Abbas Aio interrogavit Abbatem Macarium, sic: Dicito mihi aliquid. Ait ei Abbas Macarius: Fuge homines; sede in cella tua, et defle peccata tua; nec dilexeris loquelam hominum; salusque tibi obtinget.

The Scriptorium Project is the work of a small group of lay people of various apostolic churches who are interested in the preservation, transmission, and translation of the works of the early and medieval church. Our efforts are to make the works of the church fathers accessible to anyone who might have an interest in Christian antiquities and the theological, philosophical, and moral writings that have become the bedrock of Western Civilization.

To-date, our releases have pulled from the Greek, Syriac, Georgian, Latin, Celtic, Ethiopian, and Coptic traditions of Christianity, and have been pulled from sundry local traditions and languages.

APOPHTHEGMATA

Nile River Valley Church Series (Coptic, Nubian, Ethiopian):

Teaching & Discussion by St. Orsisius of Tabenna (Feb. 2008)
The Holy Ghost by St. Didymas the Blind (Sept. 2008)
Rule of St. Macarius by St. Macarius of Egypt (Apr. 2009)
Letter to Leo by St. Proterius of Alexandria (June 2009)
The Paradise of Heraclides by Heraclides of Alexandria (Apr. 2013)
Discourse on Mary Theotokos by St. Cyril of Jerusalem (Sept. 2013)
Nicene Canons in the Old Nubian Language (Jan. 2018)
First Book of Ethiopian Maccabees (Dec 2018)
Life of St. Mary the Egyptian by St. Sophronius of Jerusalem (May 2019)
The Old Nubian Miracle of St. Mena (Jan. 2021)
Two Letters by St. Dionysius of Alexandria (Apr. 2022)
Instructions: Counsel for Novices by St. Ammonas the Hermit (Sept 2022)
Religious Exercise and Quiet by St. Isaiah the Solitary (Oct 2022)
The Vision of Theophilus by St. Cyril of Alexandria (Dec 2022)
Second Book of Ethiopian Maccabees (Aug 2023)
Apophthegmata by St. Macarius the Great (Nov. 2023)

www.ingramcontent.com/pod-product-compliance
Lightning Source LLC
LaVergne TN
LVHW051922060526
838201LV00060B/4139